I0606048

In memory of Joseph, Mary, and Mindy Pactovis. —D.B.C.

For Abraham J. Peck. —K.O.

To my nieces—May Ágnes's determination as an athlete and woman always be an example to you. —M.P.

KAR-BEN PUBLISHING®
An imprint of Lerner Publishing Group, Inc.
241 First Avenue North
Minneapolis, MN 55401 USA
Website address: www.karben.com

Main body text set in Tw Cen MT Std Medium.
Typeface provided by Monotype Typography.

Image credits: Keystone Press/Alamy (top both); Peter Kohalmi/AFP via Getty Images (bottom).

Library of Congress Cataloging-in-Publication Data

Names: Cohen, Deborah Bodin, 1968– author. | Olitzky, Kerry M. author. | Peluso, Martina, illustrator.
Title: Twist, tumble, triumph : the story of champion gymnast Ágnes Keleti / Deborah Bodin Cohen and Kerry Olitzky ; illustrated by Martina Peluso.
Description: Minneapolis : Kar-Ben Publishing, [2025] | Audience: Ages 5–9 years | Audience: Grades K–1 | Summary: "Ágnes Keleti can forget about the war when she is doing gymnastics-until Jewish athletes are barred from the gym. Never giving up on her dream, her moment of triumph comes at the 1952 Olympics"— Provided by publisher.
Identifiers: LCCN 2024006478 (print) | LCCN 2024006479 (ebook) | ISBN 9798765619773 (lib. bdg.) | ISBN 9798765652756 (epub)
Subjects: LCSH: Keleti, Ágnes—Juvenile literature. | Women gymnasts—Hungary—Biography—Juvenile literature. | Jewish athletes—Hungary—Biography—Juvenile literature. | Olympic Games (15th : 1952 : Helsinki, Finland)—Juvenile literature. | International Jewish Sports Hall of Fame—Juvenile literature. | Jewish women—Hungary—Biography—Juvenile literature.
Classification: LCC GV460.2.K4 C65 2025 (print) | LCC GV460.2.K4 (ebook) | DDC 796.44092 [B]—dc23/eng/20240326

LC record available at https://lccn.loc.gov/2024006478
LC ebook record available at https://lccn.loc.gov/2024006479

Manufactured in Guang Dong, China by Dream Colour Printing
1-1010885-51800-4/24/2024

Twist, Tumble, Triumph

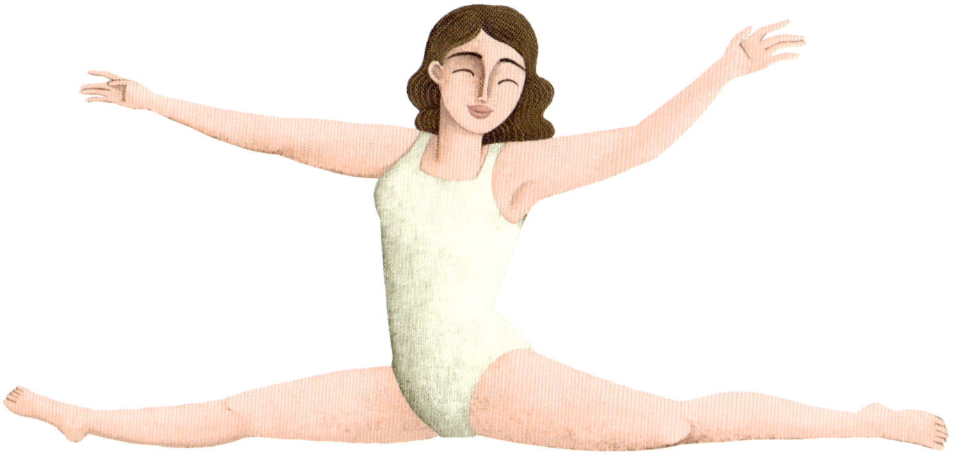

The Story of Champion Gymnast Ágnes Keleti

written by Deborah Bodin Cohen *and* Kerry Olitzky
illustrated by Martina Peluso

KAR-BEN PUBLISHING

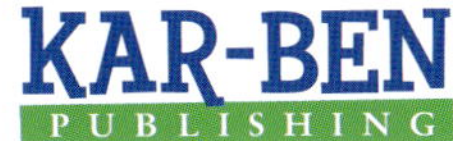

Ágnes Keleti reached for the uneven bars and took hold.

She rotated twice around the low bar, then jumped to the high bar. She felt free.

Soaring through the air, she could forget the war. She could forget the laws that made life difficult for Jewish families like hers. Looking down, Ágnes only needed to worry about landing her vault. Nothing more.

After practice, her coach took her aside.

“There’s a new law, Ágnes,” her coach explained. “Jewish athletes aren’t allowed in the gym any longer. I’m truly sorry.”

Ágnes felt her jaw drop. “What? I’m the Hungarian National Champion. This is the national team’s gym.”

Ágnes refused to beg. Instead, she imagined herself on a balance beam. Steady. She would not allow herself to fall.

Walking out of the gym, Ágnes passed a Jewish teammate, István Sárkány. He was clearing out his locker. They locked eyes, and István nodded glumly. Ágnes looked away to hide her tears.

That evening, after supper with her family, Ágnes heard a knock on the door. István stood outside.

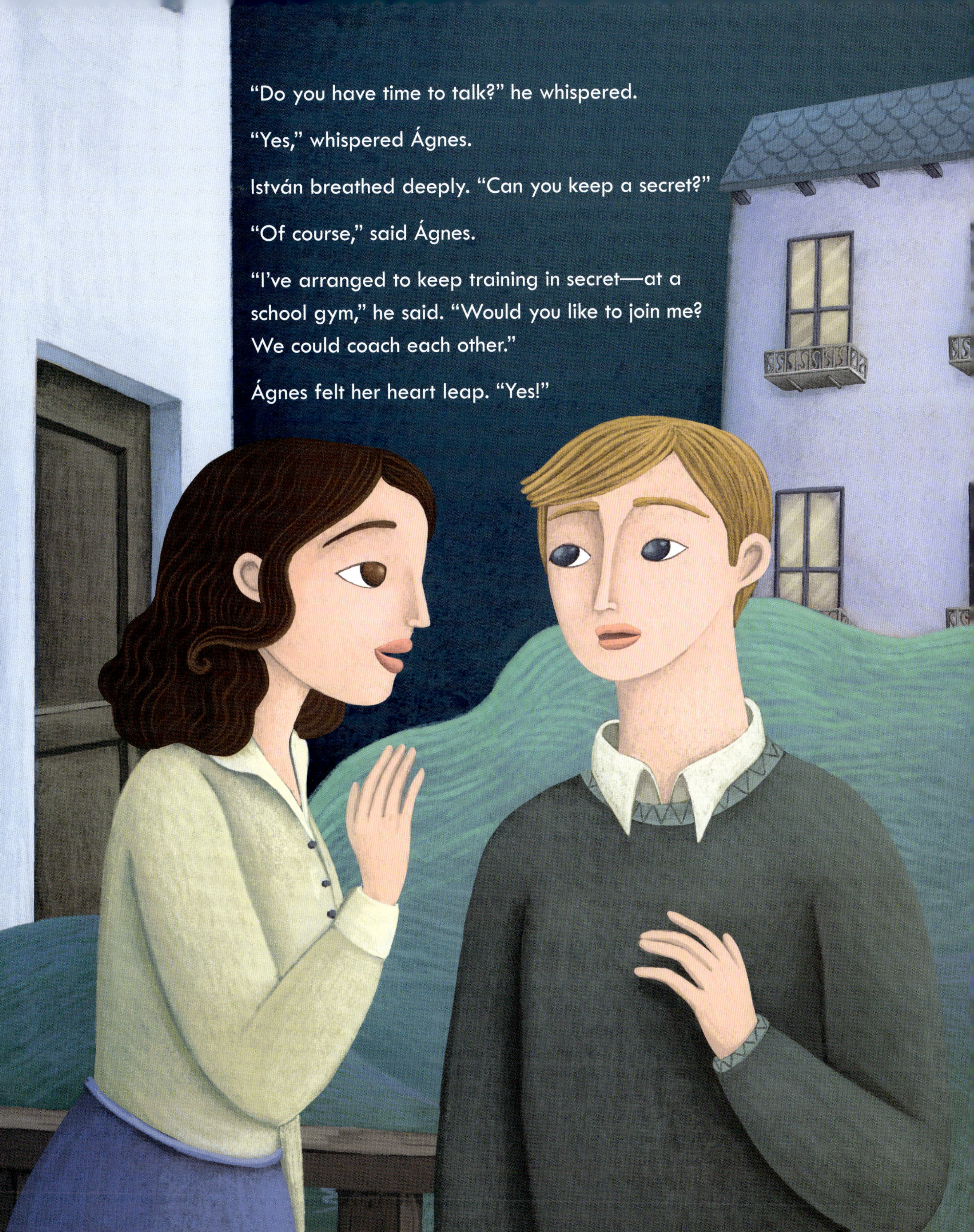

"Do you have time to talk?" he whispered.

"Yes," whispered Ágnes.

István breathed deeply. "Can you keep a secret?"

"Of course," said Ágnes.

"I've arranged to keep training in secret—at a school gym," he said. "Would you like to join me? We could coach each other."

Ágnes felt her heart leap. "Yes!"

The next morning, Ágnes arrived at the school before dawn. István appeared out of the shadows. He led her through dark hallways to a basement gym. “I don’t think there’s any heat in here,” he said, rubbing his hands together.

“It’s okay,” said Ágnes, forcing a smile. “Once we start practicing, we’ll warm up.”

It was true. As Ágnes practiced,

she forgot all about the cold.

Each morning, Ágnes met István at the school gym. There, doing tumbles and flips, she could forget about prejudice and the war.

But then Germany sent soldiers into Budapest. Nazis patrolled the streets with large, growling dogs. They were impossible to ignore.

New laws required Jewish people to wear yellow stars on their clothing. István came to practice with a star sewn onto his jacket. Ágnes said defiantly, “I won’t wear one. Why should I make it easy for the Nazis to hurt me?”

One morning after practice, Ágnes walked past the train station. She saw Nazis forcing Jewish men, women, and children onto crowded train cars. She didn't know where the Nazis were taking these people, but she knew it couldn't be anywhere good.

Ágnes hurried home and told her family what she had seen. "We must go into hiding. It's too dangerous for us here."

"Ágnes is right," said her sister, Vera.

Papa shook his head. "I have my factory."

"Please, Papa," begged Ágnes. "The Nazis don't even permit you to go to your factory anymore."

Ágnes knew that when Papa spoke in that stubborn voice, he couldn't be convinced. So Ágnes focused on saving Mama, Vera, and herself. She'd heard a rumor that the Swiss embassy had set up safe houses for Jews around Budapest.

"Vera, you and Mama can get permission from the embassy to live in one of their safe houses," Ágnes told her sister.

“What about you?” asked Vera.

“Too many people here know me as a gymnastics champion,” said Ágnes. “I need to leave Budapest so I can hide my identity.”

A Christian woman named Piroska agreed to sell Ágnes her identity papers. Ágnes would pretend to be Piroska. She memorized every detail of Piroska’s life. Then Ágnes fled Budapest.

At a checkpoint outside the city, Ágnes showed Piroska's identity papers to a Nazi guard. He quizzed her. Ágnes was terrified, but she answered all his questions correctly.

When he let her pass through the checkpoint, Ágnes felt as if she had won a gold medal.

Still pretending to be Piroska, Ágnes made her way to a small farming village. She found a job doing housework for a family who supported the Nazis. The family had no idea that their maid was actually Jewish—and a gymnastics champion. Ágnes didn't let herself react when they said something bad about Jews.

Every other Sunday, Ágnes had a day off. She swam in the Danube River, letting the cool water refresh her. She practiced gymnastics in a field.

Amid wildflowers, she did handsprings

and imagined herself at the Olympics.

She told herself, "Someday, the war will end."

Ágnes worried about her family. Not speaking to them was agony. Ágnes decided to take a risk. From the village post office, she called Mama.

"Vera and I are safe," said Mama. "But the Nazis arrested Papa. We also heard that the Nazis sent your friend István to a labor camp."

Ágnes felt dizzy, as though she had lost her balance during a flip. But she couldn't crumble in a busy post office.

"Be careful, Mama," she said softly.

"You too, Piroska," said Mama.

Fierce fighting broke out in the countryside. The village was no longer safe. Ágnes had to return to Budapest and hope nobody would recognize her. She slept in an underground shelter to avoid the bombs falling on the city. Each night, she dreamed of the war ending.

Then one morning her dreams came true: Ágnes heard a man calling joyfully, "Come out! The war is over! Come out, it's safe!"

Ágnes didn't believe him until she saw Allied soldiers giving food to people coming out of the bomb shelters. Her heart leapt. It was true! From that moment on, she left her identity as Piroska behind and became Ágnes Keleti once again.

Ágnes found Mama and Vera. Together, they returned to their damaged apartment. They stayed in the ruins and waited for Papa to return. He never came.

A cousin returned and told them the news they dreaded to hear: Papa was killed in the concentration camp at Auschwitz.

As Ágnes mourned Papa, she tried to look toward the future with hope.

One day István appeared at their door. He weighed just seventy-three pounds and struggled to walk, but Ágnes was overjoyed to see him.

"I'll get stronger," he said. "Soon I'll be ready to train again. Would you like to help me find a gym and train with me?"

"Yes!" said Ágnes without hesitation.

Bombs had destroyed most gyms in Budapest. Ágnes and István gathered equipment into a makeshift gym. Other gymnasts joined them, including some who had been unkind to Jewish teammates during the war. Ágnes didn't let herself focus on what they had done. She had one simple goal: being the best gymnast that she could be.

Within a couple of years, Ágnes won the Hungarian National Championship again. An ankle injury kept her out of the 1948 Olympics. But Ágnes remained determined to compete in the Olympics one day. She said, "I survived a war. An injury will not end my dreams."

At the 1952 Olympics in Helsinki, Finland, Ágnes marched proudly into the arena to compete in the floor exercise. Her moment had finally come.

She was thirty-one years old, twice as old as the youngest gymnasts. She had missed three Olympics: two because of the war and one because of injury. She had less than two minutes to prove herself. She needed to score over 9.7 to win the gold medal.

Ágnes breathed deeply. She nodded to the pianist and leapt toward glory. Her routine started with simple tumbles and leaps, then grew more complex. She combined strength with grace.

When she finished,

the crowd broke out in thunderous applause.

The judges wrote their scores on placards.

As each judge held up a scoring card, Ágnes slowly let out her breath. Her combined score: 9.86!

The announcer proclaimed, “Ágnes Keleti is the Olympic champion.”

After years of twists and tumbles,
Ágnes had triumphed.

And she was just getting started.

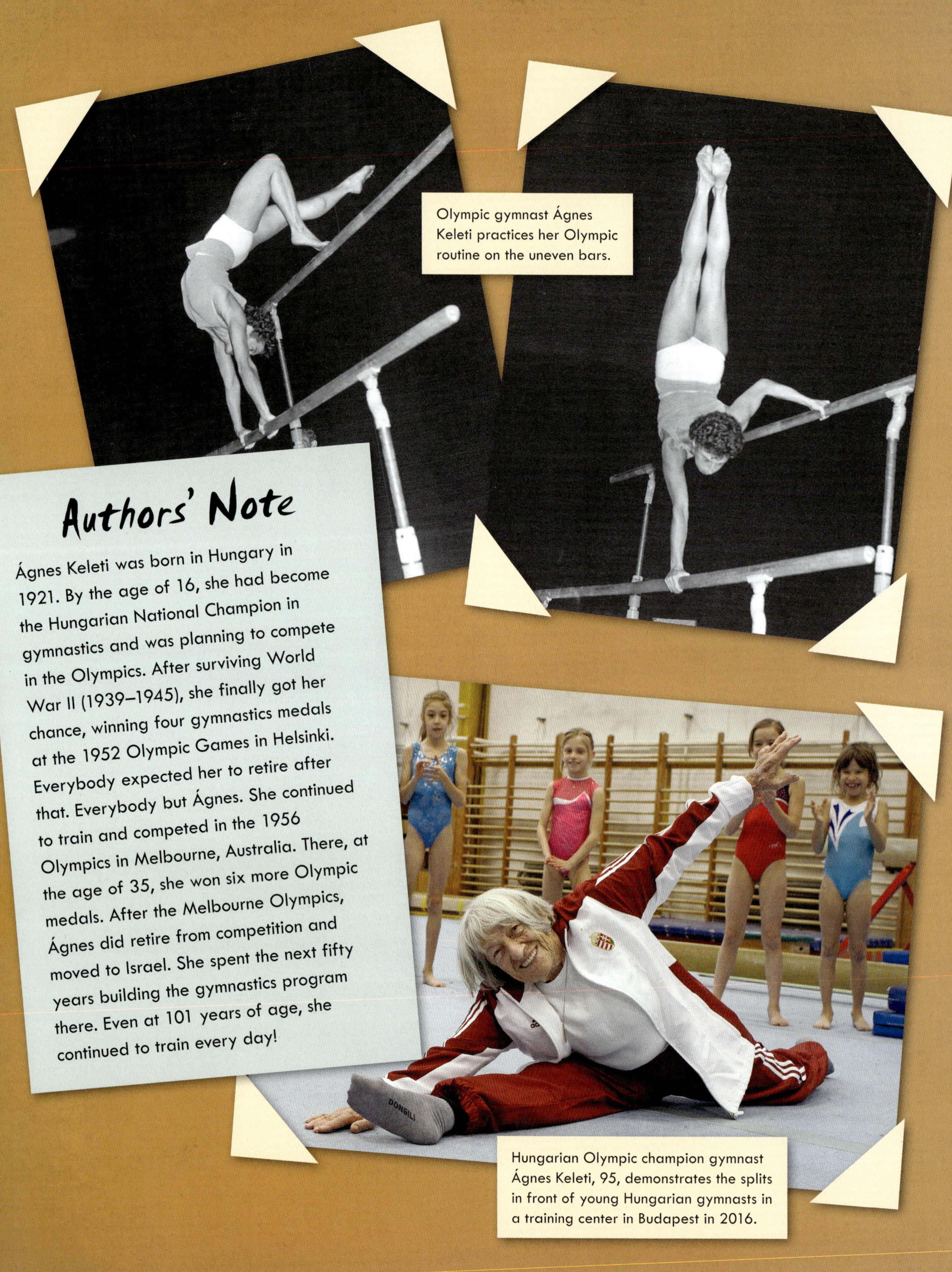

Olympic gymnast Ágnes Keleti practices her Olympic routine on the uneven bars.

Authors' Note

Ágnes Keleti was born in Hungary in 1921. By the age of 16, she had become the Hungarian National Champion in gymnastics and was planning to compete in the Olympics. After surviving World War II (1939–1945), she finally got her chance, winning four gymnastics medals at the 1952 Olympic Games in Helsinki. Everybody expected her to retire after that. Everybody but Ágnes. She continued to train and competed in the 1956 Olympics in Melbourne, Australia. There, at the age of 35, she won six more Olympic medals. After the Melbourne Olympics, Ágnes did retire from competition and moved to Israel. She spent the next fifty years building the gymnastics program there. Even at 101 years of age, she continued to train every day!

Hungarian Olympic champion gymnast Ágnes Keleti, 95, demonstrates the splits in front of young Hungarian gymnasts in a training center in Budapest in 2016.